THE QUIET COLLAPSE OF EDUCATION

Why Learning No Longer Needs Schools

But Children Still Need Humans

by

BRIAN B. TURNER

For permissions requests, inquiries, or more information, contact:
HEY BBT LLC
www.heybbt.com

ISBN (Paperback): *978-1-971050-24-9*
ISBN (eBook): *978-1-971050-23-2*

First Edition

Printed in the United States

Table of Contents

Author's Note

This is not a critique of schools.

It is a reflection on what childhood is becoming.

I am not writing this as an educator, a technologist, or a policy expert. I am writing this as a father who is watching the world change faster than any system designed to prepare kids for it.

Knowledge is no longer scarce.
Attention is.
Identity is.
Presence is.

The tools my children have access to are more powerful than anything I grew up with. They can learn almost anything instantly. They can connect to anyone. They can perform for the world.

But I am less certain they are being taught how to become themselves.

This book is not about nostalgia for the past.
It is about clarity in the present.

We are living through a quiet shift where education is no longer about transferring information. It is about shaping humans inside systems that were never designed for them.

Algorithms teach faster than teachers.
Platforms shape identity more than families.
Visibility rewards performance more than depth.

None of this is evil.
None of it is intentional.

It is just how systems evolve.

The question is not whether technology will change childhood. It already has.

The question is whether we will raise humans who can use these systems without being shaped entirely by them.

This is a short book because the truth does not need many words.

It needs honesty.
It needs restraint.
It needs reflection.

What follows is not a set of instructions.
It is a framework for thinking.

About learning.
About identity.
About attention.
About what we are really paying for.
About what we are really building.

Not smarter kids.

Stronger humans.

That is the only future I care about preparing my children for.

Chapter 1: The Future of Education Isn't About School

There was a time when school was where learning happened.

Not symbolically.
Literally.

If you wanted knowledge, you had to go to a building, sit in a room, and listen to someone who had access to information you did not.

School was not one option among many.
It was the interface to the world.

That is no longer true.

And the shift did not happen loudly.

It happened quietly, through screens, through devices, through tools that were never labeled as educational but became more effective than classrooms ever were.

The world did not announce this change.
It simply moved on.

We still talk about education as if it is about knowledge.

It is not.

Knowledge is no longer scarce.

It is abundant, searchable, personalized, and instantly available to anyone with a phone.

The scarcity moved.

It moved to attention.
To identity.
To emotional development.
To self-direction.
To presence.

The question is no longer:
Where do you get information?

The real question is:
Who do you become inside infinite information?

School was designed for a different world.

A world where:

- books were limited

- experts were rare

- learning was slow

- information traveled poorly

In that world, school made sense.

It organized access.

It created structure.

It standardized learning.

But when the conditions changed, the system did not.

It kept teaching content in a world that no longer needed it.

Today, children can learn almost anything without a teacher.

They can:

- watch lectures from the best minds in the world

- practice skills with personalized software

- explore subjects at their own pace

- ask questions without embarrassment

- repeat lessons endlessly

Not because schools failed.

Because tools evolved.

And tools always reshape behavior.

So what is school now?

Not a learning engine.

A social environment.

A place where children learn:

- how they are seen

- how they fit

- how they compete

- how they withdraw

- how they perform

- how they protect themselves

School became the place where identity forms.

Not knowledge.

And identity is far more powerful than information.

This is why debates about curriculum feel increasingly disconnected from reality.

We argue about what should be taught while children are already learning everything elsewhere.

What they are not learning elsewhere is:

- how to exist among others

- how to manage rejection

- how to speak without fear

- how to handle boredom

- how to fail publicly

- how to build confidence slowly

Those are human skills.

And school quietly became the primary place they are practiced.

Education did not disappear.

It changed form.

It moved from:
content to context
information to identity
knowledge to self-concept

We just never updated the language.

The future of education is not about better schools.

It is about understanding that school is no longer the center of learning.

It is the center of becoming.

And that distinction changes everything.

Chapter 2: Knowledge Is Free

There was a time when knowledge had a gate.

You had to go somewhere to get it.
You had to know someone who had it.
You had to wait for access.

Information lived inside buildings.

Schools.
Libraries.
Universities.
Institutions.

If you were outside those systems, you were outside learning.

That structure shaped everything.

Today, knowledge no longer has a location.

It is not stored in rooms.
It is not controlled by credentials.
It is not protected by systems.

It is searchable.
Translatable.

Repeatable.

Instant.

A child with a phone has more access to information than a university student did twenty years ago.

Not because the world became smarter.

Because the world removed the gate.

We still behave as if information is scarce.

We still design systems around:

- delivering content

- transferring knowledge

- standardizing instruction

But content delivery is already solved.

Quietly.

Through:

- videos

- forums

- open courses

- AI tutors

- digital libraries

The world built a parallel education system without calling it one.

The real bottleneck moved.

It moved from access to attention.

From knowledge to motivation.

From information to self-direction.

Two children can now live in the same house and receive completely different educations.

Not because they go to different schools.

Because one learns in private and one consumes in public.

This is the shift most people miss.

Education is no longer limited by:

- resources

- teachers

- institutions

It is limited by:

- focus

- discipline

- curiosity

- emotional stability

Those are not academic skills.

They are human ones.

When knowledge becomes free, success no longer depends on what you are taught.

It depends on what you choose to engage with.

And choice is shaped by:

- attention

- emotion

- identity

- environment

Not curriculum.

The old divide in education was structural.

Who had access.
Who could afford it.
Who was allowed in.

The new divide is internal.

Who can focus.
Who can think alone.
Who can build slowly.
Who can resist distraction.

Who can sit with complexity without escaping into noise.

We often say the internet democratized knowledge.

That is true.

But it also privatized responsibility.

No one decides what you learn anymore.

Not your school.
Not your teacher.
Not your parents.

You decide.

And most people are not trained to decide well.

This is why so many people feel overwhelmed by information instead of empowered by it.

They are not lacking knowledge.

They are lacking direction.

And direction is not something you download.

It is something you develop.

Knowledge is no longer the product of education.

It is the raw material.

The real skill now is not learning.

It is choosing what to learn, when to learn, and why.

And that skill is almost never taught.

Chapter 3: School Is a Social System, Not a Learning System

We still talk about school as if its primary purpose is teaching.

It is not.

Not anymore.

That function moved elsewhere.

School now exists for something different.

Something less visible.
But more powerful.

If you removed every test, every syllabus, and every lesson plan from school, something would still remain.

The social environment.

The human system.

Children do not just learn subjects in school.

They learn themselves.

They learn:

- how they are seen

- how they compare

- how they fit

- how they are treated

- how they respond to authority

- how they manage rejection

- how they protect their identity

Those lessons are not in the curriculum.

But they are the ones that stay.

Most adults do not remember what they were taught.

They remember how they felt.

Who ignored them.
Who embarrassed them.
Who chose them.
Who excluded them.

Who believed in them.
Who made them invisible.

School is remembered emotionally, not academically.

Because it trains the emotional system first.

School is a forced human environment.

You do not choose the people.
You do not choose the structure.
You do not choose your role.

You are placed inside a system and told to adapt.

That is not about learning information.

That is about learning who you are in relation to others.

Every day in school is practice for:

- speaking in groups

- navigating hierarchy

- managing boredom

- handling conflict

- performing under observation

- responding to failure

- existing inside authority

These are the skills that shape adult life.

Not grades.
Not credentials.
Not test scores.

But the ability to function inside human systems without losing yourself.

This is why AI cannot replace school entirely.

AI can teach faster.
It can personalize perfectly.
It can remove embarrassment.

But it cannot:

- ignore you

- challenge you emotionally

- exclude you

- misunderstand you

- test your boundaries

- reward your courage

- punish your silence

Those experiences are human.

And they are the real curriculum.

Schools still describe themselves as learning institutions.

But their actual role shifted.

They became social calibration systems.

They sort children into:

- leaders

- followers

- outsiders

- performers

- rebels

- observers

Not by intention.

By structure.

And those identities often persist for decades.

We measure schools by outcomes that barely matter.

Scores.
Placements.
Admissions.

But the real outcome is invisible.

Does this environment produce:

- confident humans

- emotionally stable adults

- people who can speak

- people who can listen

- people who can stand alone

Because that is what school actually creates.

Not knowledge.

Humans.

Education did not collapse.

It evolved into something we never named.

A social system pretending to be a learning one.

And that quiet shift explains more about modern childhood than any curriculum ever could.

Chapter 4: AI Tutors Will Outperform Classrooms

This is the part most people resist.

Not because it is false.

But because it challenges something familiar.

The idea that one human in a room can teach twenty-five children better than a personalized machine already feels outdated.

We just have not admitted it yet.

Classrooms were built around a single constraint.

One teacher.
Many students.

Which means:

- one pace

- one explanation

- one style

- one timeline

Everyone adapts to the system.

Not the other way around.

Some children are bored.
Some are lost.
Some pretend.
Some fall behind quietly.

This is not a failure of teachers.

It is a failure of design.

AI does not teach like a human.

It teaches like a mirror.

It adapts to how you think.
It repeats without frustration.
It changes explanation style.
It slows down or speeds up.
It remembers where you struggled.

It does not assume you are average.

It treats every learner as unique.

That alone makes it a fundamentally different system.

In school, feedback is delayed.

Mistakes linger.
Confusion compounds.
Understanding stacks unevenly.

With AI, feedback is immediate.

Errors are corrected in real time.
Gaps are identified instantly.
Learning becomes smoother.
Less emotional.
Less shame-based.

Which matters more than people realize.

Most children do not hate learning.

They hate feeling stupid in public.

A great teacher can change dozens of lives.

A great AI system can change millions.

Not with burnout.
Not with fatigue.
Not with turnover.

Just with iteration.

The best explanation in the world can now be copied infinitely, improved constantly, and personalized endlessly.

That is not a threat.

That is progress.

Most great teachers already do this instinctively.

They adjust.
They repeat.
They notice gaps.
They personalize.

AI simply does it at scale.

This is why the shift is irreversible.

Systems that are:

- cheaper

- faster

- more personalized

- more available

always win.

Not because they are better morally.

But because they are better structurally.

Education is no exception.

People often reject AI tutors because they feel impersonal.

But the irony is that most classrooms are already impersonal.

Twenty-five children.
One pace.
Minimal attention.
Limited customization.

That is not human-centered.

That is logistical.

AI is the first learning system built around the learner, not the institution.

Schools will not disappear.

Teachers will not vanish.

But the monopoly is over.

Learning already moved.

Quietly.
Individually.
At home.
On phones.
On laptops.
In private.

Classrooms were not replaced.

They were bypassed.

AI tutors will not replace schools.

They will replace the learning function of schools.

Which means schools will have to finally admit what they already became.

Not learning engines.

But human development environments.

And that is not a downgrade.

It is simply a different role.

Chapter 5: The Social Cost of Optimization

Every system eventually learns how to become more efficient.

Education is no different.

We remove friction.
We personalize content.
We optimize performance.
We accelerate progress.

And slowly, something human disappears.

Not because anyone intended it to.
But because efficiency is not neutral.

It shapes behavior.

When learning becomes perfectly optimized, it also becomes emotionally thinner.

No waiting.
No boredom.
No awkwardness.
No public mistakes.
No social risk.

Everything becomes safe.
Private.
Controlled.

Which feels better.

But does something worse.

Human growth depends on friction.

Not intellectual friction.
Emotional friction.

The kind that comes from:

- being misunderstood

- being ignored

- being challenged

- being embarrassed

- being excluded

- being seen

Those moments hurt.

But they also form:

- resilience

- identity

- boundaries

- confidence

- emotional range

You cannot build those in isolation.

Optimization removes discomfort.

But discomfort is where development happens.

This is the paradox of modern systems.

The more efficient they become, the less human they feel.

Not because they fail.

But because they succeed.

Children now grow up inside environments designed to reduce risk.

Algorithmic feeds.
Personalized content.

Private learning.
Curated communities.

Everything adapts to them.

Very little challenges them.

They are protected from:

- silence

- boredom

- rejection

- waiting

- being wrong in public

Modern systems reward visibility faster than competence.

Children now grow up watching people become successful by being seen, not by becoming skilled.

The lesson is subtle but powerful.

Perform first, develop later.

Which feels compassionate.

But quietly weakens emotional muscles.

We often say technology empowers.

It does.

But it also insulates.

From:

- social tension

- emotional ambiguity

- unscripted interaction

- unpredictable feedback

Which are exactly the experiences that produce mature humans.

A child who only learns in optimized environments may become:

- highly competent

- highly informed

- highly skilled

And still feel:

- socially fragile

- emotionally avoidant

- uncomfortable with conflict

- dependent on validation

Not because they lack intelligence.

But because they lacked friction.

This is the cost of optimization.

Not loss of knowledge.

Loss of emotional texture.

Life becomes smoother.

But thinner.

More efficient.

But less formative.

The danger is not that children will become less capable.

It is that they will become less resilient.

Less tolerant of discomfort.
Less patient with others.
Less comfortable with ambiguity.
Less able to stand alone without feedback.

We are building systems that remove pain.

But pain is part of becoming human.

Not suffering.

Not trauma.

But the small, daily friction of existing among others.

Without it, growth becomes clean.

And clean growth is fragile.

The future will be filled with people who know a lot.

But may struggle with:

- rejection

- boredom

- conflict

- silence

- being unseen

Not because they are weak.

But because the systems around them removed the experiences that once built strength.

Quietly.

In the name of progress.

Chapter 6: What Parents Are Actually Paying For

Most parents believe they are paying for education.

They are not.

They are paying for environment.

They are paying for:

- structure

- standards

- peers

- expectations

- social norms

- daily rhythm

Not content.

The content is already free.

Any child can learn:

- math

- science

- history

- languages

- coding

- finance

Without leaving their bedroom.

That is not what tuition buys.

Tuition buys a context.

When parents choose a school, they are not choosing a curriculum.

They are choosing:

- who their children spend time with

- what behavior is normalized

- what ambition looks like

- what success is modeled

- what failure feels like

- what values are reinforced

They are designing a social ecosystem.

Not an academic one.

This is why two children can attend schools with identical rankings and have completely different outcomes.

Because the invisible curriculum is different.

The culture.

The expectations.

The emotional climate.

Parents rarely say:
"I want my child to be surrounded by disciplined peers."

They say:
"I want a good school."

But what they really mean is:
"I want an environment that shapes my child in a direction I believe in."

This is also why expensive schools feel powerful.

Not because the teaching is better.

But because the signal is stronger.

Children absorb:

- what is normal

- what is expected

- what is possible

From the people around them.

Not from textbooks.

Every school is a social filter.

It selects:

- who belongs

- who leads

- who speaks

- who feels safe

- who is invisible

Those filters shape identity more than any lesson plan.

This is the part no brochure explains.

Parents are not purchasing knowledge.

They are purchasing:

- peer influence

- cultural alignment

- behavioral modeling

- emotional environment

They are outsourcing part of their child's identity formation.

Whether they realize it or not.

Which means the real question is not:
"Is this school academically strong?"

The real question is:
"What kind of humans does this environment produce?"

Confident or anxious.
Curious or compliant.
Independent or dependent.
Grounded or performative.

Those outcomes matter more than grades ever will.

Most parents sense this intuitively.

That is why they tour schools.

They are not evaluating syllabi.

They are feeling the energy.

The tone.

The social temperature.

The unspoken rules.

Because deep down, parents know:

You can teach a child anything.

But you cannot isolate them from the environment that shapes who they become.

And that is what they are really paying for.

Chapter 7: Designing the Hybrid Child

The future is not human or machine.

It is both.

Children will grow up with tools that think, respond, generate, predict, and adapt.

They will not remember a world without artificial intelligence.

To them, it will feel like electricity.

Invisible.
Everywhere.
Normal.

The mistake is to ask whether AI should be part of education.

It already is.

The real question is how.

The old model of education separated learning from life.

You learned in school.
You lived everywhere else.

The new model dissolves that boundary.

Learning happens:

- in private

- on demand

- inside tools

- inside systems

- inside algorithms

Life becomes the classroom.

And the classroom becomes optional.

This does not mean children will become less capable.

It means capability will become easier.

Which shifts the real work.

From learning to becoming.

The hybrid child is not someone who replaces humans with machines.

It is someone who uses machines to free humans.

To free:

- time

- energy

- focus

- emotional bandwidth

So that what remains is human.

AI will handle:

- repetition

- memorization

- practice

- feedback

- simulation

- exploration

Humans must handle:

- values

- boundaries

- meaning

- identity

- courage

- emotional development

The machine can teach skills.

It cannot teach character.

The danger is not overusing AI.

The danger is outsourcing identity.

Letting algorithms shape:

- attention

- motivation

- self-worth

- social comparison

- life direction

Without conscious design.

A well-designed hybrid child grows up with:

High cognitive leverage.
Strong emotional core.
Comfort with tools.
Comfort without them.
Ability to learn alone.
Ability to exist among others.

Not dependent on systems.

Not hostile to them.

Just grounded inside them.

This requires intention.

Not policies.

Not platforms.

Not institutions.

Parents must design environments where:

- tools are used, not worshipped

- performance is visible, but not rewarded blindly

- progress matters more than metrics

- silence is not feared

- boredom is allowed

- discomfort is not avoided

Because those experiences shape identity.

Not software.

The hybrid model is simple.

Let machines optimize learning.

Let humans optimize becoming.

Anything else reverses the order.

And the order matters.

The goal is not to raise children who can compete with AI.

That is a losing game.

The goal is to raise children who can use AI without losing themselves.

That is the only future worth designing for.

Chapter 8: Raising Builders in an Algorithm World

The future will belong to people who can build something when nobody is watching.

Not content.
Not a brand.
Not a persona.

Something real.

Algorithms reward visibility.

They reward performance.
Reaction.
Speed.
Engagement.
Being seen.

But none of those produce meaning.

They produce attention.

And attention is not the same thing as value.

A builder is different.

A builder works in silence.
Learns without applause.
Improves without feedback.
Fails without an audience.
Continues without recognition.

Not because they are disciplined.

But because they are aligned.

The world will teach children how to perform.

It will teach them:

- how to be interesting

- how to be noticed

- how to optimize themselves for systems

- how to convert identity into output

It will not teach them how to sit with themselves.

How to think alone.
How to wait.
How to persist.
How to build slowly.
How to choose depth over speed.

Those must be taught intentionally.

The real danger is not that children will become artificial.

It is that they will become fragmented.

Pulled between:

- metrics

- comparison

- validation

- noise

- endless feedback

Until they no longer know what they actually care about.

Builders are not immune to technology.

They just do not let it decide who they are.

They use tools.

They do not outsource identity.

They create.

They do not perform existence.

Raising builders does not mean raising entrepreneurs.

It means raising humans who can:

- define their own goals

- tolerate silence

- survive boredom

- work without praise

- learn without pressure

- exist without an audience

Those skills will matter more than any credential.

The systems around them will always change.

Platforms will evolve.
Tools will upgrade.
Careers will mutate.
Markets will shift.

But a person who can build something meaningful from nothing will always be relevant.

In any economy.

In any future.

The goal is not to protect children from algorithms.

That is impossible.

The goal is to give them something stronger than algorithms.

A sense of self that does not depend on being measured.

A life that is not optimized for attention.

A mind that can choose depth over dopamine.

That is what I want for my children.

Not success.

Not fame.

Not advantage.

But alignment.

The ability to live inside powerful systems without becoming shaped entirely by them.

To use technology without letting it define them.

To build quietly.

And to know who they are, even when nobody is watching.

A Quiet Note to Parents

The world our children are growing up in will not slow down.

It will become faster.
Smarter.
More efficient.
More personalized.
More automated.

They will have tools that can think for them, predict for them, recommend for them, and optimize nearly every part of their lives.

They will never experience information scarcity.
But they may experience meaning scarcity.

They will never lack access.
But they may struggle with direction.

They will be surrounded by systems designed to guide them.
Shape them.
Measure them.
Reward them.

The challenge will not be helping them learn.

It will help them remain human inside systems that do not need them to be.

The future will belong to those who can use algorithms without becoming them.

Who can benefit from powerful tools without letting those tools decide who they are?

Who can exist in a world of constant feedback without needing to be constantly validated?

Who can build something real without needing to perform their existence?

That is what I want for my children.

Not advantage.
Not perfection.
Not protection.

Just the ability to live inside powerful systems without being shaped entirely by them.

To think clearly.
To feel deeply.
To choose deliberately.
To build quietly.

And to know who they are, even when nobody is watching.

That's the whisper.

No hype.
No summary.
No lesson.

Just a human closing the loop with another human.

This page is what turns the book from *philosophy* into *legacy*.

www.ingramcontent.com/pod-product-compliance
Lightning Source LLC
Chambersburg PA
CBHW022342280326
41934CB00006B/751